EXTRA
ILLICIT
SONNETS

EXTRA ILLICIT SONNETS

GEORGE ELLIOTT CLARKE

EXILE
editions

Library and Archives Canada Cataloguing in Publication

Clarke, George Elliott, 1960-, author
Extra illicit sonnets / George Elliott Clarke.

Poems.
Issued in print and electronic formats.
ISBN 978-1-55096-498-1 (paperback).--ISBN 978-1-55096-499-8 (epub).--
ISBN 978-1-55096-500-1 (mobi).--ISBN 978-1-55096-501-8 (pdf)

I. Title.

PS8555.L3748E97 2015   C811'.54   C2015-906554-2
                                                C2015-906555-0

Published by Exile Editions Ltd ~ www.ExileEditions.com
144483 Southgate Road 14 – GD, Holstein, Ontario, N0G 2A0
Printed and Bound in Canada in 2015, by Marquis Books

We gratefully acknowledge the Canada Council for the Arts, the Government of Canada
through the Canada Book Fund (CBF), the Ontario Arts Council, and the Ontario
Media Development Corporation, for their support toward our publishing activities.

Canadian Sales: The Canadian Manda Group, 165 Dufferin Street,
Toronto ON M6K 3H6 www.mandagroup.com 416 516 0911

North American and International Distribution, and U.S. Sales:
Independent Publishers Group, 814 North Franklin Street,
Chicago IL 60610 www.ipgbook.com toll free: 1 800 888 4741

À Colette

À Pushkin

Contents

Enjoy a video of George Elliott Clarke speaking about the book,
his style of "blank" sonnets, and the transcendent wonder of words.
Scan, or via URL at: www.tinyurl.com/ClarkeEIS
(11:00)

Both faces leaned together like a pair
Of folded innocents, self-complete....
There seemed no sin, no shame, no wrath, no grief.

—Elizabeth Barrett Browning

The poet makes Beauty *by pondering the* Real.
How else is born the act of Love?

—Simone Weil

Old woman, Eros can arise....

—Jane Munro

I

POETRY

Performance

I like to fuck, and hold forth on fucking,
For I hold fucking dear. I like to love
As nakedly as I write. How do I
Muster up *Poetry*? My love scratches
In her *Crisis*; I scratch paper with ink—
A sonnet of grunts, a ballad of moans—
Blacking up poetry that blanches prudes.
We total the sheets as we culminate.

When my love's absent, I can't join my heart
And lungs to words. I need our tongues sponging
Each other, our thighs lunging, composing
An epithalamium that's all groans—
Wedding-night cries, wriggling—giggly, then gasps,
And nary a dumb ejaculation!

(I begin this *Chronicle* with fucking
Because that's how you, sweet *Reader*, began!)

—*Luca Xifona**

---

*This Vancouver, B.C., jazz saxophonist, Canuck, of Libyan-Maltese her-
itage, penned this erotic exotica while recording *Red-Hot, White-Hot, Black-
Ice Blues* (2015), his debut.

Honest Sonnet

I'm a "vulgar scribbler"? So what?
Truth raps nasty, tapping dew from sewers.

A hypocrite is an imposter saint,
An apostate apostle. That's not me!
I'm too antsy, my fancies too fanatic.
I don't shy from explicit *Sleaze*, posh *Filth*.

(Bid lustrous bottles bring on clustered mouths,
Then bodies wrangling in *Indecency*!)

Ecclesiastical curses, verses
Smutty as Catullus, emphatic as
The Vatican, that's what I write: Trouncing
Jane Austen, but jouncing Anaïs Nin.

Poets know *Love*'s notorious for *Lust*:*
Dirt abounds—like birdsong—as *Love* is made.

---

*Thus, the Marquis de Sade's ancestor, Laura, inspired Petrarch's sonnets.

Late, Late Renaissance

When I'm as immobile as Shakespeare's bones—
Or a has-been poet, my pidgin tongue
Echoing a brooding pigeon, my skull
Skinned marble smooth or rust-tin crushable,
My poems will still speak the clarity
Of *Misery*, because my cot's driftwood
Without her anchor, or my room's a cell—
Bereft of her virtuoso *Nudity*.

(Eden needs hedonists—tireless lovers,
Who doth holler *Time* into submission.)

The muffled copulation of angels
Doesn't suit me, serpentine, strumpeted:
I need my love luxuriously shouting—
Wet ink trumpeting *Love* in fourteen lines!

Composition

Could I couch you in a cushion of ink—
Posh, nocturnal words—and picture you, white,
In black letters, on a white sheet—a white
Candle inflaming night, shaming moonlight,
I'd be that love poet that poets think,
My lips pouting, trying to spell or spout
Passion and *Lust* clerks know fuck-all about,
To draft your *Beauty* no reader shall doubt.
Woman of sun-gilt frost, hardly can black
Verses limn snow limbs, fire hair, sky-blue eyes:
How can dark ink scribe starkly silver thighs?
(*Metaphor*'s a mirror—opaque at back.)
Your bright breasts flutter two white butterflies:
English tints *Black* when *Beauty* testifies.

II

TIDING

Spontaneous Insight

That door, now hinging on light, saw sun spring,
Bingeing, as you alighted. I eyed smiles
Warming winds otherwise freezing Rodos.
Sixtyish vixen, tits biting your blouse,
You acted, cool, cerebral, a Socialist
Spinster, an elderessa playing mum.
But you spilled your shadow over my wine,
Leaned, laughing, braless, over my writing:
Quite flustered, I lusted; sighting *Lustre*.
You caught me looking. A stinging glitter
Benighted my sight. I dreamt our flesh meshed:
I'd cleave thy cleft til sonorous closure.
Love coagulated like lightning, a storm
Striking Rodos: I felt each seizing stroke!

Early March, Rodos

Proud Rhodians out of Rhodes.

—HOMER

Even the orange blossoms were complicit
In *Titillation*: Spume—winds—forged perfumed
Orgasms, minting that citrus *Spring*,
Lighter-than-air, of Rhodes, hinting *Something*....
    Dramatic, you traipsed a gossamer scent
Through Rodos' lemon-and-orange blossom air....
    Elder, "retired" from *Love*, you thought yourself
Consigned—confined—to a commune of nuns,
And repressed your small-breast *Glamour*,
Delicates delegated neath denim.
    (But *Travel* crafts will-o-wisp relations:
Couples uncouple mid untangling limbs—
Or wordless lips—a mockery of tongues.)
    March it was, but the brisk breeze smelled April.

Interpreting Luca Xifona

I don't know him. I saw him watching me—
Lingering like a shadow, or trailing
After my "scent" (though I wore no perfume):
His prowling moves proved as sleek as *Silence*.
　　Each chrome-pale dawn, each grape-blushed eve, musing,
He viewed me as the portrait of a prize.
　　(Women are, to men, abstract *XXX*—
As mysterious as *Algebra*'s x.
I know these truths undermine *Romance* myths.)
　　Under Rodos' wintry palm trees, his wish
To kiss me—an ordinary lady—
Seemed a black gesture. I knew he was wed.
　　Solitary, he craved *Adultery*,
A menacing *Seduction*. I knew it.

—Sonia Fuentes *

---

*Sonia Fuentes, a native of Andorra, is a literary translator specializing in Catalan, Spanish, French, and English. Her preferred novels are Whodunits, not "Let's-do-its."

Tarnish

Strange, incandescent Luca,
silver-sugar-lunged man,
I think you think your heart bleeds clean—
pure as 24-carat gold:
But I spy a taint—
that black char of infernal *Lust*.

A devilish god, an *Evil*-besmitten angel,
perhaps you harangue weak-flesh women
with such poetic pizzazz (*Jazz*),
they sprawl before you,
open to baptism.

You sport a boyish, joyous mask,
but were you ever truthful,
your very lungs would be transparent,
just too clear for you to breathe!

You rise from a demon's murky abode
to invade nymphs' innocent spheres,
emitting dirty light, pulsing sweaty heat,
O cunning traveller! Diabolic Odysseus!

III

INITIATION

Rapacious

You were not expecting that kiss—sudden
Summit of tongues: "Oh!" marked your dazed outcry.
After our tongues see-sawed as one, our talk
Teeter-tottered. But a gust of giggles
Prefaced plaited whispers. We clinched again—
To elongate ejaculate *Pleasure*.
Not a one-time, once-upon-a-time kiss—
While rain washed wind with bold, cold ash—I felt
Exuberant as a gull, thrilled to be drenched!
I clenched your undulant smallness. You guessed
My filthy *Imperative*: To entrench
My sex while tongues romp—Frenching—euphoric.
Then, blossoms dispensed *Insolence*—their sparks,
And, next eve come, fresh leave had we again.

Andorran Seduction

Memory knows, *in vino veritas.*
Thus, I sound the bottle's abject bottom....
To honour Rodos—mosquitoes, high winds—
I emptied dark wine into your white flask.
    In tango heels, you were *Standing Woman*;
But—now—*Nude Reclined*, while wine bottoms out,
Then tops up. Bacchus—god of wine—pours vats.
Each gulp we take shakes bright as meteors.
    Andorra is "Pyrennial" mountings!
Each screw uncorks a *Paradise* of pours—
And never any bitterness at the lees,
The untimely *Climax*.   A white-and-black
Duet, we roar in sheets—as if hived bees,
Until we breathe honey—mead—and we drown.

Stanzas Written in Reflection

I.

My sugar-silver nakedness
Was your dream, *al fresco*,
In Rodos, where we found ourselves,
Talking—a year ago.

Were we mumbling culprits, flirting
Over ale, numinous
As lunatics? Springtime *was*—but
Not I—"promiscuous."

Bitterly, you walled off yourself,
Acted a haughty poet,
A standoffish chap, ignoring
My entrance, my exit.

In truth, amid blurry moonlight,
And palms, the sea's murmur,
And jugs of lemony, Greek wine,
I schemed for no lover.

My *Passion* moot, my breathing pale;
Your *Bonhomie* crafted:
I was pure pelt, teeth, and gristle,
Not lusting for your bed.

To live and breathe *Sex*, its sizzle of
Surprise, unto bland chill,
Or seal my lips upon your lips,
To kiss and kiss until....

Was not my agenda! Never!
I felt our age difference.
Perhaps pimps lisp, "Aged gals fuck best?"
False! "Old gals" value friends.

II.

If I'm a wan and wavering woman,
I'm content to nip at *Delights*, not gulp.
But you came laughing—guffaws, not titters—
And talking poetry and pouring *rosé*....

To Luca

You've drilled a vein—
broken through;
sunk a shaft—
steaming, greasy,

to my core—
mother lode,
pure pitch of riches

only you can mine

(all mine)

or stake or pilfer—

finding yourself ever
voluptuously repaid—
the deeper and dirtier you get—

in the blessed going in
and coming forth.

@ Paris

But there was the old, old problem:
Should it be celibacy, matrimony or unchastity?
—EDGAR LEE MASTERS

I've come to hilt you across tilting waves,
That damned Atlantic that divorces us.

Married, I'm an angel—but with dead wings.
Loving, I feel *élan*—to the *éclat*....

So, our couch sees dank *Swank*—glinting pools
Of sweat and wine, while fog swallows each night.

I feel lustful, blunt, as curt as *Hunger*,
Asking that we twine like writhing spring snakes.

(The oddest *Warmth* wafts up as we scrunch down,
Twixt sheets, flinching like pinched butterfly wings.)

To live is to sin. Vows break lavishly.
Our City of Light winks at—shades—*Affairs*:

We're not the first two to deceive a third.
Look: Sacré-Coeur, white, peeps at red-light whores.

Amsterdam

Rain is threads of tears—weaving, unweaving,
Lacing panes, stringing leaves, til Amsterdam's
Shimmering as sassily as whitewash.
Ashen canals, glimmering, drain off murk.
Night comes in, rain thrums—redundant
Abundance; dwindling leaves bolster the wet.
Scarlet lamps garnish salty, sea-smoked *Smut*—
So we spy out harlots in the worst light.

Later, we'll return to rooms, to gossip
In chairs, then undertake *Love*'s rustic work,
Pressing out incessantly drizzling wine.

The bed's glimmering ground is ours—our bare
Experience, our *Joy* that gleams, while ooze
Unfurls, jets us wet and shameless as *Grief*.

Amsterdamned

A withering gale strips down Amsterdam:
The trees lurk now, pared down like sex workers.
Leaves rain into the October canals,
While red lights inflame these watered-down reds.
    You tongue my tongue, then hand me old pictures—
Black and white snaps of you, white and dark-haired—
Bust bared—as your photographer lusted.
I ogle eye-goggling *Anatomy*.
    Then you are stripped and lie—sterling silver—
Scarlet hair leafing flame over cream sheets—
While my lips breathe blossoms upon your lips.
    Rain pelts our hotel's windows as my thighs
Pelt yours (or *vice versa*): *Vice* versus vows.
I'm still my wife's husband, but withering.

To Luca (II)

Our *Love*'s "a black, anarchist *Spectacle*—
Matching Red Guard Maoists who smash statues"?
No! It's "drowsy bebop, as our thighs swivel
And pivot in syncopated *Revelry*"?

Nay, I've—it's true—a proud, *Bestial* fetish:
To gloat over our coltish arias—
Our whinnying epics! Yes! I do all
A dog does, on all fours, just as you like!

Nothing's more natural than animals,
And what we do, coupling, sets me neighing
Or snorting—hyperbolic—like a nag!

Let's bog down in musk, hog each other's flesh,
Gripe only when *Climax* halts us, panting—
Exhausted like a felled king's *Treasury*.

IV

"GENEALOGY OF MORALS"

To Sonia

I use your name here, declaring a bond,
A trust, though I should not—because I can't,
Being foresworn to another, just as dear.
But *Love*'s larger than *Law* and's not contained
By vows or script. But yet, how can I vow
Any veritable *Affection* if
I'm false to her I'm already ascribed?
How can you trust my vows untrustworthy?
　　Indeed, I'm only script—a sheet of words
Sliding before your eyes as stealthily
As I slide beneath your sheets when I can.
And yet, I vow, I'm true—these words show true:
If I violate one iron commandment,
I keep another—just as adamant.

Struggle

The first command is "Breathe!" But the last is
"Repent!" Each new heartbeat wants *Love*; each breath,
Aged instantly, yearns as it faints, until
Death abruptly incarnates "*Corruption.*"
    Too sad a gospel is that, I believe....
Don't be inhuman, inhumane, hurtful:
That's enough scripture for *Love* to obey.
    My spouse, envious Venus, espouses *Hate*:
I'm "solely lousy," to love who I shan't.
But I looked at you; you at me: We saw
An exculpatory *mea culpa*.
    We know *Pain*. There's one apocalyptic *Cure*:
To kill our *Pain*, we should murder our *Love*....
    Impossible! *Light* medicates our room.

Venetian Ceiling

Under our Venetian ceiling, we look
More apes than angels and, at *Lust*, as black
As the demon sent sprawling planet-ward,
In that sky-view painting* above your bed.

His wings are reptilian; his tail daggers
In an arrow aimed at heavens too bright
For his species, as he falls toward us,
Where we sprawl, untidily, looking up.

One angel, above us, shows bold, proud breasts—
Shameless, sinless—and she, saintly, ignores
The plummeting devil, and us—"fallen,"
But your form is sunlight's earthy *Eclipse*.

Vraiment, we stew as sodden as is Venice—
Love yielding downpours, dew, and atmospheric mists.

---

*A hotel room *copy* of Giambattista Tiepolo's ceiling in the Tiepolo Room in Ca' Rezzonico. His art allegorizes *Nobility and Virtue Defeating Perfidy* (1744-45).

"Death of a Ladies' Man"

My wife swears I possess a "rat-tail tongue,"
That I lie—just so I can "lie with dogs
Or sleep with pigs." "Appalling in each lung,"
Says she: I "bray like asses stuck in bogs,"
To declare *Innocence*, my "trifling prayer."
"Like a tent-show Sade," I'm pure *Rhetoric*—
"Seductive," but unproductive of "plaisir."
I'm a "satyr," if not "satiric."
    Her punishment isn't sluggish: She yearns
To thrust a splinter up my urethra,
To prove *Love* just a cockamamie con.
    I dug a grave of *Guilt*; she flays my gilt—
I'm "Robespierre's shade," a "sybaritic Don Juan":
I should be supine, suited in grave silt.

V

"JUST LIKE STARTING OVER"

Of Marriage

Marriage is a sinuous prison—as
We both know, having before been married,
And lived that parentheses of *Penance*—
Households, howling—mid curlicues of babes.

Marriage is a lick—a slick—of honey
In a hog's head of vinegar. That's not
Our *State*—singles, who remain singular,
Yet twined, twinning sugar and licorice.

I prefer *ex cathedra Ambrosia*,
Plain, as when your squeals shatter the bedroom:
My mouth sips your tongue; your sex slips up mine.

A borderline husband-and-wife, that's us:
Our bona fide *Intimacy* is proof!—
Akimbo and nimble—like newlyweds!

"Marrying"

If we're married, for each, it's our third time.
If we're married, it's without a wedding.
If we're married, it's without strict bondage.
If we're married, it's our favoured *Marriage*.

No woman can love and not act as *Wife*—
To have savage cleaving, such gaping *Bliss*:
I feel my legs are wings and that I fly.
In bed, embedded, we are wedded twice.

Joy is *Justice*—I mean, us, justified,
Flouting every dictate of *Church* and *State*,
And holding court—disrobed—with smelts and ale.

Alone, we're only two unlit candles.
As one, we strike a sun-lit universe.
If we're not coupled, there is no *Heaven*.

—S.F.

To Luca (III)

Is my talk sugared enough, salty enough?
I really don't know how to seduce a man.
I wonder how other women do it?

Is it really just a matter of hiding one thing
and showing a bit of another?

Well, I'm guileless in my styles.
I don't dress to entice.
Yet everyone's surprised when I state my age!

Is it ale that makes a man lewd,
that grafts him "beer goggles"
so he'll screw any opening?

Is it perfume that tempts?
A *Chanel* strategy?

I wish I knew!

Imperative!

Feast thee now on succulent crab and *Sekt*—
Or veal and port, and set thy throne in sack.
The beetling second-hand of the clock-face
Times not *Love* that's diurnal *and* timeless.

I've traversed air, oceans, and snow, to come,
Twitching and gritty—Samson as flotsam—
To shimmy our limbs, and refresh our *Glee*,
With you, Sonia, dirty as Delilah.

Celestial beings, we've come—bestial—to earth:
I know that *Nurture* stems from my rooting,
Churning, seeding of your moist, plush, hot sex—
Flourishing heroics for our *Georgics*!

Or I'm a matador dancing flamenco;
Or copper earth quaking, collapsing, thy snow.

Sermonic

Beauty ignores dust, plus everything blear
Or bitter. What is dressed in dust is dead—
As is flesh waning in phthisis. *Beauty*
Favours *Fiesta*, not desert, not ice.
(*Hell* is coffins—beings gone to scraps, scrapings
Of dirt. The dead beatify *Decay*.)
    I savour our jolly rooting—rutting,
Truculent, that unbuckles *Luculence*.
We cavort in sunlight and sport in shade.
Our conjoint flesh—disjoint in counterpoint,
Is appropriately tidal, fluxing,
For *Sympathy* cycles with *Rivalry*.
    Let's translate Tantalus to Catullus:
To cease to wish and never wish to cease.

For My Companion

Accompany me, bonny companion—
And spring up sweets, gush milk, and ooze honey—
And make our singleness a mutual
Compact that we doubly dissolve, coupled.

Solo, we're sundered; but as two, we're twinned,
And no more drift, but rendezvous, rooted
In our routing—our outing to a room,
That we've charted extremities to claim....

So many letters—too many letters—
Have passed—and pass—between us, echoing
Spectral moaning, a substantial yearning,
That's dissatisfied in its *Satisfaction.*

But we're vapours, save we anchor ourselves,
Merging in our converging parallels.

To Luca (IV)

Luca? That's another name for *Sunlight!*
You're no hand-me-down lover, some slave
Who's bought and sold, cashed in, carried off
By whomever's smile boasts more false gold....
    No doubt, you could chase a covey of beauts—
Harlots of bad childhoods, but good build—
Born gum-cracking, pony-tailed prostitutes.
Careful: *Infections* damn these undammed sluts!
    At each foul, bold-face bitch, I snarl, "He's mine!"
Thus, my legs, chopstick-thin, tweezer and squeeze
So tight, you can't escape.... You're free no more!
Our bones mirror us til the sob of dew.
    See! My sinuous whiteness ignites—flares—best
In your Pushkin shade, your bronze gusto.

In Our Garden

As flexible as grass before a scythe,
You bend to me; I bend to you: *Pliant*.
The blade is *Time*, as usual, or it's *Love*:
Both bring us falls; both bring us yields. We yield.
   A feasible blessing is our downfall—
Our windfall—*Ether*-sweet—for each other.
   Your gardener's touch privileges flowers,
Petals of mounting tingles and spasms—
Breaths and sproutings—that bring us blameless *Bliss*.

—*S.F*

VI

BEATITUDES

Of Sonia

My heart-woman is Sonia, no other.
Her mouth is sweet; her you-know-what is sweet;
Her breasts are sweetbread; her thighs are sweetmeat.
She is champion ivory, doubled cream.
To couple her is to porch in an orchard—
To pass from Wonderland to Neverland—
To plum and milk, pear and cheese, cake and port—
Impactful *Happiness* in one compact.
Steeped liqueur's her cream *Nakedness*, enough
To nudge, nerve, and animate the poet
Who claims her love, to clamour much, sleepless!
Nirvana's made flesh when *Love* is wanton,
So dew beflowers each limb, and nothing is
Sorrow, save the parting after pairing.

Delirium

I want a scalding day, when sheets are waves,
And your body is water and mine is boat,
And we shiver caught in a sirocco,
Mutual, so we clutch at foam and froth.

Andorran *femme*, you're at home with peaked ice,
But are volcanic, tense, immense with fire.
And when you're tabled in sack, I find flesh
As wet as wine, furious to be downed.

Your lips, agile, don't saunter: If sugar's
Communication, if I want sweetness
Incessant, gulping, like a sculptor hungry
For a woman who is untamed marble—
Manna, measured freshness, yielding firm snow—
A light burning nocturnally, I come.

Singular Visionary

How many visionaries see as we see—
How *Love* surfaces, two faces form one
Foundation, surfing upon each other,
And two-backed *Sex* backs mirroring *Beauty?*

I see you as sugar ministering
To my pepper, sweetening white my sheets—
Plus my black-inked sheets. May's blossoms ignite,
So you light my darkling muck's *Imagery....*

Was *Beauty* born when you were born? Or *Love*
Only? Needed I years to learn to love.
Yet, my eyes spied your *Beauty* right away,

Among rain-taste grapes and sun-bright lemons,
Your undammed perfume damned me, fuming *Lust*,
Until you—true *Innocent*—saw me plain.

Valentine

My spry and sprightly *Valentine*,
So dynamically serpentine,
Your spiced furrow I will harrow,
Milking *Nectar* from the marrow.

And when I triumph in your silk,
Spreading ecstatic streams of milk,
And then percussive *Rutting* pause,
Our climax to fresh *Coupling* draws.

Elite, erotic elderess—
(Amply, damnably damp in dress)—
Now more wife than ever mistress,

You free Venus when you unleash,
Thy beloved and bewitching niche—
Quim—just I justify.... *Capiche?*

VII

ODYSSEYS

I—Berlin

A bolt of sun were you—blazing, striking—
Jolting aside the greyed light cascading
Into Berlin's airport, as I set down,
To ravish, relish, and rapture your *queynte*
As many times as three nights could permit.
   Thrilling, earthy, not ethereal, you were
Much more ludic than lewd: Bone-and-flesh real.
   How sunny you looked as I left little
White clouds upon your belly—the symbols
Of my unstopped *Desire*—those salty pools
Of milk or snow. My jets set you jesting,
"You've made me all wet, inside and outside."
   When we parted two days later, sweat coursed
Our skin—alive like sunlight, as it rained.

II—Berlin

Gratified by our feast—*salmagundi*
Cooked torrid in mortar, you were juicy
As a *kissel*, delectably creamy
As it is finished, gratifyingly.

Our compliance with *Lust* isn't grudging.
We even tolerate the small rupture
That's *Climax*—trumpets rearing like cobras....

Love is exclusive as *Conspiracy*—
Or it's wet *Math*, a vast, exponential
Gluttony that totals all speech and thought:
It's fresh wine pouring—splashing old wine out!

I'm no more reticent than is a bull!
My profile's copper where yours is fine chalk.
We burn like oil paintings drunken with fire.

I—Rome

What is Rome without our love? Only ruins.
Our city's this couch—the Coliseum
In miniature and roaring afresh.
We eye sackings wherever the Pope prays.
No *Good* comes ever from The Vatican—
Unless our love's invoked in prayers. (Preachers
Prove despicable buggers, for they grant
Platonic *Love* no room but hindquarters!)
Andorra's peaks show snow, but august Rome's
August-hellish, so we slurp *gelato*,
Quaff copper-coloured ale, to help cool down
Our Infernal City as it burns up.
If *amore* is light more real than Roman
Marble, then there's no empire outside us.

I—Morocco

The spreading turbulence of the waves hurtles
Us on to Morocco, pitching through dawn,
Til Ceuta*—that harbour's homely suction—
Affords us sheltering wetness, mooring.

Next up's a Bazaar—a dusty tangle
Of butchers (their short-cut *Art*) or bankers
Or barker-coyotes (half-fox, half-fraud):
Our purses get rent like lambs mined for meat.

We feed now on currency, not currants—
So cash and perfume course in lush tides, if
Not quenching the mart's trenchant, startling *Stench*.

Light's at a premium where goods are hawked
That repay gawking, only if we pay,
Commanding banked coins to countermand *Greed*.

---

*Pronounced "Zewta" (rhymes with "Utah").

II—*Morocco*

Our Spain-bound boat flouts the streaked, gilded main,
Veers to Gibraltar, pushing silver foam,
While Morocco dims to shadow and dream
(Merchants keening, peddling gold amid gloom).

As confrontational as a mirror,
The sea's opposing surface (part sapphire,
But one part tar, like bursts—splashes—of *Raki*)
Glares at us, flares light's sober, surly flush.

Now we crumble dull monuments of waves—
Morocco rendered ruins—to clutch at mist,
Cinematic shadows, silk-sheer, *Porn*-blear.

Gaze at crinkling, pallid, appalling seas—
Each deepening surface, and then submit
To nurse my horse, to feel—galloped—a mare.

I—Malta

All-conquering, August sun batters down
As hot as a sauna. Malta blazes
Like molten stone; is dull like stone. We meet
A daily summer, all torrid amber.
    Dulled winds, panting, make no difference—or shade.
The fiery sky cracks each heart that's dry stone.
The heavens—molten gold—saunter and burn.
Our somber thirst coughs up a desert sea.
    Drinking breezily, we down draughts of mead
To pacify this thirty-degree heat,
Where dust is—no miracle—instant flame.
    In our cool sheets, we cry out as if scorched,
Only then have we thrilling shivering,
And gasping *Atonement*, and sweat that's rain.

II—Malta

Water bright as puddled aluminum—
Sunlight striking silver out of turquoise—
My Malta's *ours*: Gold-leaf stone, gilded heat,
The Inquisition ebbed to hellish tours
Of white, anti-refugee infernos,
Where sweat bakes on shadeless Gozo, or sears
Eyes blind. To flout the heat, we flee the beach
To chow chilled rabbit, quail, ale, and mead.
    Our *Genius* is the ruckus—when we rout,
Stress, our Maltese mattress, our podium
Inspiring improvised *Lyricism*.
The air-conditioner, emotional,
Rasps jealously at our zealous loving.
But our body heat's our *Rebuttal*.

III—Malta

The snowy boiling of Maltese froth—
A volcanic broth, sour, nocturnal malt—
And rippling rain, all night, whip up street dirt....
But: No distaste in licking our skins' drops!

Our glad palavering sets quavering
Our limbs—like a bee at the pinnacle
Of follicles, setting a flower crooked.

I'm seasick from the earthquake of your thighs—
The equestrian leaping of your seat:
We delve deeply in berserk, jerking sheets.

Your mouth opens; your "*Lolita*," white purse
Opens; both are sundered, plundered, left creamed.
My *Devotion* doesn't deviate:
That's "your" penis, love, in "my" vagina.

I—Puumala

Vineyards overtake our kitchen; white wine
Yields invisible ink; black ink flashes
Just like pepper; here night is twilight, charred
Indigo, with indigenous *Lustre*.

Smoke surges as if to purge pale *Blackness*—
That pointless, desolate tint, these white nights
Of jettisoned gleam, of stars run aground.
Rain cascades as raucous as tin, peeling.

Frost-prone Finland, this summer, deigns we don
Blankets as shawls, sport boots for shoes, and stroll
In lightning abrupt as a guillotine.

I'll tap thy gap; but first, I'll unwrap thee,
Silvery, elven, diluting blackness,
Dismantling night, our bodies being candles.

II—Puumala

The sauna fire is a cantering blaze;
Wetness grants us a sugary finish.
We ladle out morsels of water that
Hit hot stones as an overhanging splash.
Steam foams up, then vanishes in fresh sweat—
A drifting *Beneficence*, or silver
Effusion: We both bathe in fusing light.
    The leaping strike of water on scorched stones—
The burst of it—equals a squall, a storm
Of phosphorescence, as do you, a-bunk,
When I'm burnt stone and you are cool water.
But there's no fog in our union, no mist,
Save our gasps, ballooning us to "*Cloud Nine.*"

III—Puumala

Along berried ground, that semi-marine
Bush, bog, bright with butterflies, near shady
Water, we step—slog—inescapable
Venus and inexorable Cupid—
Loving to tumble and clench and couple
Prodigiously, in our steaming tumult,
In the sauna, where drips shine upon us
Like drizzled steel.

Already, woman, you're a sizzling well—
Your bones radiant under encircling
Sunlight, my *Kalevala* nymph or sprite,
And I'm thy inked, incandescent bard.

You cut a green trophy—the birching leaves—
And thrash us with overjoyous tremors.

II—Rome

Again roam we to Rome, again we come,
Again to know *Love*, and this time to spy
Shelley and Byron and Keats in their graves,
Parlayed into marble and violets.

It's with macabre *Prudence* that we love:
From cloudy start-ups, through intermittent
Heartache and long-suffering pulse, until
That muted *"Eureka"* that starts our deaths.

Yes, Rome is more eternal than our flesh
And will welcome new loves once we're forgot,
Unless our words thrive—like the stars—deathless.

So this poem is resonant with other
Love poems, conspiring against *Time*'s tireless
Corrosion—if *Composure*'s impassioned.

VIII

RETURNS

Sweets

To cherish cherry kisses, and to pluck
From nimble limb, or nest of lips, and suck
On every cheery dish that nourishes—
Is what every choice lover cherishes.

I was too disciplined when I embraced
First loves. (But dull a chaste diet does taste!)
I was afraid to reveal my needing
All the *Joy* that was there for my feeding.

But the body's best a corpse, if it fails
To cleave to others. Unbearable jails—
Or alarms—of *Morals* imprison us,
Til candied *Coitus* comes to poison us.

I want no sweets labelled—libelled—by *Threats*
And *Regrets*. Cherish sweets one gives and gets!

April 16, 1977

    Her blonde hair blazed sun-hot against her green
Sweater—or coat—wool that thickened her waist
Falsely. I reckoned her thinness beneath
And poured purple honey—*Manischewitz*,
As we sat on the beach, under the stars,
On the cold sand, lips pursing, while *Song* hissed,
Sashaying out my *Sony* tape player.
Near midnight, flirting, my arm hooked her waist.
    That was a child's *Virginity* ending:
Our *Bliss* pushed us unto *Maturity*—
Desire, Deviance, Discharges, Dissent.
    We loved. I think we loved. But, foolish me,
I wasn't ready for such *Love*. No, no—
Not until, decades later, you and I kissed.

April 19, 1981

Under the willow tree, in April wind,
Her brown hair almost joined those whipping fronds,
As her lips scrupled to sculpt Saxon words
As cool and crisp as The Queen-graced dollar.
    I felt I loved her, but didn't dare say,
Fearing I'd scare her off. I just acted
Stern and aloof, but her jesting came warm:
Her *Innocence* seemed Del Jordan-actual.
    But she was woman, never *Muse* or *Myth*,
And wholly, virtually *Virtuous*,
Wanting *Contentment*, though not *Conception*.
    I mistook her *Virginity*, forsook
For jealous *Voluptuity*, corrupt,
Once, in fact, her *Chastity* was ruptured....

Selective

Do we remember the flesh visceral—
When we recall whom, when, and where we've loved
Or touched or guffawed fond, foolish, giddy
With *Pleasure* and its plush satisfactions?
    Often, there's dark port and white nakedness—
Your angular beauty, your curves swerving
Away from clothes, while the moon swings from clouds,
Darling, or the sun leaps up from the sea.
    Hotly, we swig sweat in our pet kisses
As you pull me on you, and there I ply,
While apple blossoms pelt white an orchard.
    My silver-breast sylph, sun-necklaced in gold,
Mine own "Lady Sonia," I recall best
We are lovers who rest but seldom sleep.

IX

UNIONS

Saturnalia

Like a boar in corn—wrecking, havocking,
Feasting, that's us, satisfying each pang
And demand of *Hunger*, each twinge and twang—
Uninhibited—of belly and maw.
    Our kinetics ain't aesthetic: We're beasts—
Famished and fierce. *Lust* is wild *Gluttony*,
Uncontrollable, inconsolable—
Intolerable rutting and glutting....
    Our raunchy flanks, our ratcheting haunches,
Take to thoroughbred romping and trampling,
Quaking—breaking, freakish—the creaking bed.
    Kisses cohere til we're incoherent—
Snarling, gasping, hissing. We tug each other
Toward the dessert, to taste *Sweetness* as one.

Portrait d'une femme

How you made my back buck as if a bull,
As I rode you hard; you got ridden hard,
Thigh-driven into mattress or headboard,
While our sexes tacked—or, better—smacked
Loudly, as pubis struck pubis as if
Warring. You laughed at our shenanigans—
The percussion of clash, crash, and *Climax*,
Our fussing flesh fracturing boards, leisurely—
To the point of bad joints pressured apart.
Measure for measure, you gave as you got.
Lady Chatterley and Mellors never
Experienced *Venery* so feverish,
Nor have I known any lady so
Unlady-like, as to make love like Eve.*

---

*Cf. Elle Devyne in *Fresh* (1998), dir. Guillermo Brown.

Horseplay

Galloping in our throes, you spurred me well,
Dashing the divan, splintered most to bits.
Your haunches' ornament, I was well worn—
Like a saddle, then worn out: a stud horse.
As stable—or as unstable—as sand,
That's us, as you thrash or I stamp, or growl,
My nostrils flared. I'm crucified in slosh
Once we subside, til I'm stabled again.

If I am steel, you are sinuous—silk,
As strong as steel; your reins are demanding;
Our two forms rock—rococo and raucous.

Our bodies pace—iambic, trochaic,
Anapestic, dactylic, spondaic,
But never pyrrhic, no, not until *Death*.

Horseman

I want to make love as if I have hooves
And horn, and bray in brazen, Maltese must!
Slick *Sangria* down our throats. Pitch your ass
Twitchingly in heat, your flanks, quivering.
　　I prefer you bitch, not some *Puritan*,
To drip hot and honest as a filly,
So our breathing stinks as natural as a zoo,
And our slippery joints waft skanky scents!
　　You scratch, bite, but don't slap, and I'm grateful:
Your "animal" being bears no *Animus*.
Hear my snorting breath! Your kisses retort!
　　Am I more animal than poet? Yes:
I want to couch with you until the grass
Is an antique forest all about us.

Making It

We are divine *Imaginings*, even
In our brutal carousing, our brusque love,
Our shouts tracing profane zigzags—crooked
Halos. Our bodies bash and trash all *Sleep*.

We do taunt Hell with our dauntless Heaven,
My knees pressed to my breasts, so I mimic
A Picasso model, silver in *Age*,
Pearly in face and thigh. Lo! You become
Bullish, tilting at my coral matrix,
Corralling me: We thud and slam *ensemble*.

Do be as recalcitrant as a stud
Worrying a mare, so our raunch trenches
Horses' stench, viscous, visceral groping,
Us merging insurgent bones, silk sinews.

Thy Spear

Admirable, blunt-tipped, gilt spear—
your kingly sceptre—
that cavalier erection,
that bronze tulip—

you should gird as *Treasure*—
secure, select,
according *Pleasure*
only to th'*Elect*—

this singular woman
you *must* love *singularly*!
Ignore girls' starving eyes and purring lips!
Don't spend your currency,

willy-nilly,
on any nag, mare, or filly,
who wants to prance, pace, as your mount.
Don't dream of a *Harem*,

or settle for a stable:
Fuck only me—as much as you like.
Ram your Eiffel Tower deep, deep,
to crowbar wide my Fort Knox!

Obedience

Sweet, little lamb who loves a buttery,
Battering ram, you ask, "Do I obey
Enough?" Well, you've donned silk, but have nothing
Beneath. *That's* a blessing without disguise....
Teasingly pleasing, you scoop your nightie,
Then let it droop. I glimpse what imps desire.
Obey, you, while I bay hard *Frustration*:
My "point" would come to your quaint "edge" right now!
Now, your legs—like a table's—spread, beckon,
And I drop, foam's troubadour, to spelunk
Your surf, surging, until my own surf's purged,
And wet, rinsing to our bones, scours us pure.
You are obedient when you agree,
At chafing crescendo, to make love—*not just once.*

Race

Hectic, disgusting, breathlessly, we strive
To demolish we two! To polish *Filth*!
Our pallet's best as driven sludge—warren
Of a lustrous snake squishing through a gash.
Disobedient, rebellious woman!—
God imagined Judith just so, like you—
As horizontal—right now—as the sea.

Hoochie coo *frau*, full of brine and *brio*,
Our gasps clasp, and no clench goes unanswered:
Our bundling limbs slap under trundling sheets.
Our drama's equestrian—wild and rabid—
Pounding profoundly four thighs together—
But closing with comic—wedded—spasms,
As if Othello's cast in *l'Histoire d'O*.

Holy Creatures

Oh woman, I love it when you become
That breathless, inevitable animal*—
Jumbled, a tangle of lipstick and silk—
Writhing, clutching, panting, biting, scratching—
So I hunch over odours—milky, smoky,
Nocturnal bride, limitless, limbs stretching,
Fetching, rustling up *Paralysis*,
So close to *Death*, but short-lived: *Ecstasy*.

And let us say, if we bill, squawk, and peck—
We're secular as pigeons, our murmurs—
Sacred, brooding—and our nest a shambles.

But shouldn't we be as ardent as gods—
Or ape jungle beasts' savage appetites—
And rend *Qualms* and chains like chintzy cobwebs?

Lust keels her sex so heels lift overhead.

Two Staying Abreast

Unforgettable tits bobble like foam,
While you jolt—*Conqueress*—astraddle me.
I see the blue veins of each trim, milk breast
Converge—like lightning strikes—at your nipples.
I love the downward swing of each separate,
Satin pursing, as you lean over me,
Taking my upthrust self where you're enthroned;
Your hair and tits, dipping, buffet my face.
Strip to your flash self: High spirits, cheekbones,
High heels; and next two tiny nipples tipped
Up to my tongue: Here's unveiled *Zest*, all mine!
   Your two tits are two cups at which I drink.
(*Nude*, you fuck up all protocols.) Siren!
Look! A black snake rises between your breasts.

Enjoyment

Significant *Flesh*, sugared *Love*, that's you—
Instantaneous Venus—scorching voice
Crackling my pillow, then kindling the dusk,
Your thinness being exaggerated *Light*.

In Malta—or Venice, desperate for you,
I gobbled down booze and slobbered out prayers,
Strolled by crunchy, disobedient tides,
Craving your guaranteed *Luxury—now*!

To enter a sinful Heaven—that's right—
No more squalid tears or squander of breath—
But to wed unceremoniously:
To have you shanghaied, shellacked, and swooning!

Once we're astonishing, indecorous beasts,
All else is conspicuously superfluous.

To Luca (V)

Time makes precarious our delights:
There's never enough of either.

Time outlives, outlasts, and outcasts dreamers.
The best time? Your soft stroke on my soft parts.

And yet, darling, often you're better able to talk
Than fuck; so what's romantic turns domestic:

To buss goodnight and drift to sleep, coupled
Like spoons, our fingers twined like fork tines.

I smile to recall the times you call me your *Love*,
Your *Passion*, how you'll fuck me "hard, very hard,"

But then TV news—or a movie—arrests your eye,
And/or you gulp too much *sake* and/or vodka,

And then I slip your glasses off, turn the TV off,
Turn off the light, and turn to hug you, snoring.

X

ARS POETICA

Absent Her

I keep a blacked-up, erotic diary,
But too pure still where pages lie vacant:
What can I write, if not her raptured sex,
What *Love* bares? Absent her, my pen's *Kaput*.

Sanctified cadences, that's *Poetry*:
To evaporate *Theology*,
Preferring Byron's aegis and Shelley's writ,
Until stars vanish and dew rouses grass—
And our *Passion* sets us eyeless as Milton.

Disembodied from our names, we're one flesh—
Such matched, intransigent *Magnificence*.
But, absent her, sobs scratch—like thorns—my throat.
All is *Error* if she's not here. *Sans elle*,
There's no *Reality* that isn't *Dream*.

To Luca (VI)

My poet, you blurt *Love*,
but—really—spurt *Lust*!
My pruning eye

pores over your florid inklings
only to spy wry and earthy
violets—

or hot, tottering sunflowers....
Is your *Love* gilt trifles—
or truffles,

found neath cold ruins' ashes?
"Nothing forbidden and all forgiven":
That's the "whore-to-*Culture*" sense

of your priapic blooms,

transplanted to me, thy Muse.

Still, Venus indulges
Priapus and Bacchus....

Composing

If I were only vaguely memorable—
A late-night, sugar-mouthed (bastard) poet,
My lewd face trickling liquored overtures,
Willy-nilly *Nihilism*, carnal grunts—

Still I'd sing as our limbs compose smart lays:
Play fucks up, fucks over, *Philosophy*
(That ink puddle of opaque words)—
Beauty that exhausts *Vocabulary*....

The shouted whisper of a turning page
Is as intangible as *Love*, but hear
Two bodies turn in sheets, undulating;
Now, ink pictures us in clear black and white.

Breath's vile outside our visceral *Rapture*.
When we climax, *Death*'s annihilated.

Of "Lady Sonia"
à la manière de Baudelaire

"Lady Sonia"—sylph, milf, gilf—I never
Have enough of you, nymph—elusive as
Virtue, self-evident as *Sin*, your sighs,
Stifling prayers, slur toward dove-like purring.

I desire to indulge *Glitter*—your black
Satin dress set ablaze by crimson hair
As fluid and articulate as flame—
Also wet-snow flesh, sinews of diamonds.

Beauty despoiling bedazzled poets
Of their metaphors, erotic Venus—
Your white-lightning skin drips milk-white nectar—

Fuck after fuck, as I relish the *Bliss*
Of a poet mauled by his Muse, and sprawl
With gold *Joy* in white sheets, yelling, "More! More!"

To Luca (VII): A Duet

S: We're not wedded, but coupling marries us:
Bit by bit, evenings slide into the sea,
And dates pass away until we date again.

  (*Time* is a stubborn current; it holds
At bay the docking of our crafts, or turns
Us back until its tidings favour us.)

L: Usually, like martyrs' articulate
Ligaments, we're rent by *Distance*, so speech
Turns, guttural as Pentecostals, to tears.

  Dawns come a tenebrous—then tenacious—blush
As we remain so lewdly voracious,
Trying to finish off our solitudes.

S: Let us die nakedly—*la petite mort*—
Lie together until—*stilled*—we lie more.

Touching

When we are near, what is dear is touching.
Precarious is *Solitude*, too close
To *Loneliness*, when one can't dare to touch,
For no one is near, and no one is close.

No clothing is carnal—not wool, not silk—
Unless it's touching you, and you're clutching
Onto me, and I'm touching carnal silk—
Coveting—covertly—overt *Clutching*.

Alone, far, I'm a monument of tears,
For you are distant, and your touch remote.
Sordid magma, searing are my plague tears:
My heart's a volcanic island, remote.

An *Inferno* roils my ribcage, my heart,
Tears can't put out—lest *yours* touch—*clutch*—my heart.

Notes

The Browning epigraph is from her epic poem, *Aurora Leigh* (1856). The Weil epigraph is from her *Notebooks*, Englished by Arthur Willis (2004), but under revision here. The Munro epigraph is from her verse collection, *Blue Sonoma* (2014). The Homer epigraph is from his *Iliad* (ca. 900 B.C.E.) as translated by Robert Fagles (1990). The Masters epigraph is from his *Spoon River Anthology* (1915), a lyric epic. The drawings herein and on the cover are the gifts of Claire Weissman Wilks.

Happy imagination—or idyllic hallucination—inspired this poem cycle. (*Illicit* means *irregular*.) The "sonnets" were edited in Berlin (Germany), Krakow (Poland), Halifax (Nova Scotia), Andorra-la-Vella (Andorra), Smiths Cove (Nova Scotia), and Toronto (Ontario) between March MMXIII and August MMXV.

Do these verses echo my *Illicit Sonnets* (London UK: Eyewear, 2013)? Do Luca and Sonia mirror/marry Laila and Salim? *Peut-être...*

Barry Callaghan, Pamela Mordecai, Riitta Tuohiniemi, and Paul Zemokhol edited and/or advised. For any errors, I alone *must* stand corrected.

Some of the poems herein debuted online in *Maple Tree Literary Supplement*[.ca], and in print in the now-defunct, *Descant*. Repeated here, they appear deviant. (Thanks are due, even so, to the editors.)

Merci to the University of Toronto's E.J. Pratt Professorship for merciful grants permitting me to jet hither and thither, through every type of weather, to jet these poems, that do not dither.... Yet, the Professorship is duly acquitted from any allegation of approving any dubious morality here.

I thank Michael Callaghan, Nina Callaghan, and Exile Editions for their belief in this book. I pray that you, complicit *Reader*, have found it precipitously solicitous of the felicitously *illicit*....

George Elliott Clarke
Nisan MMXV

George Elliott Clarke's many honours include the Portia White Prize for Artistic Achievement (1998), Governor General's Award for Poetry (2001), National Magazine Gold Medal for Poetry (2001), Dr. Martin Luther King Jr. Achievement Award (2004), Pierre Elliott Trudeau Fellowship Prize (2005-2008), Dartmouth Book Award for Fiction (2006), Poesis Premiul (2006, Romania), Eric Hoffer Book Award for Poetry (2009), appointment to the Order of Nova Scotia (2006), appointment to the Order of Canada at the rank of Officer (2008), and eight honorary doctorates. He is a pioneering scholar of African-Canadian literature and is the E.J. Pratt Professor of Canadian Literature at the University of Toronto, having previously held posts at Duke University and McGill University. With poetry translated into books in Romania (2006), China (2006), and Italy (2012), Clarke was appointed a Visiting Professor at Harvard University (2013-14) and Poet Laureate of Toronto (2012-15).